NATIONAL GEOGRAPHIC

What's My Job?

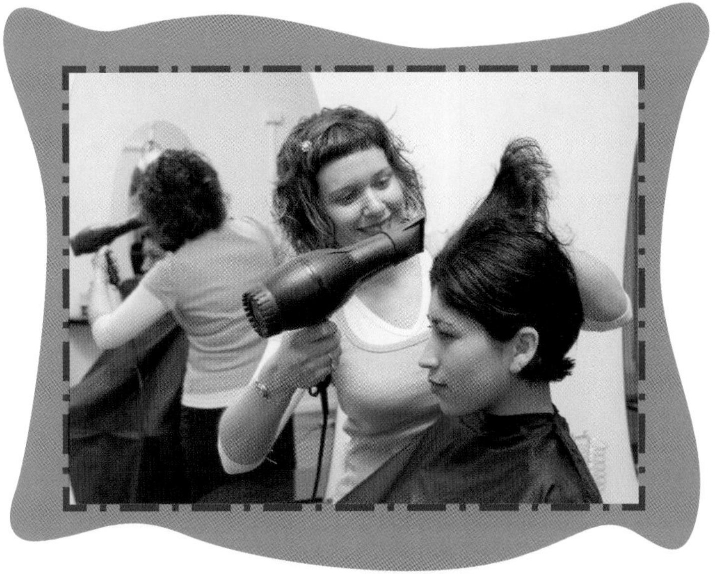

Jacob Fink

I use a comb.

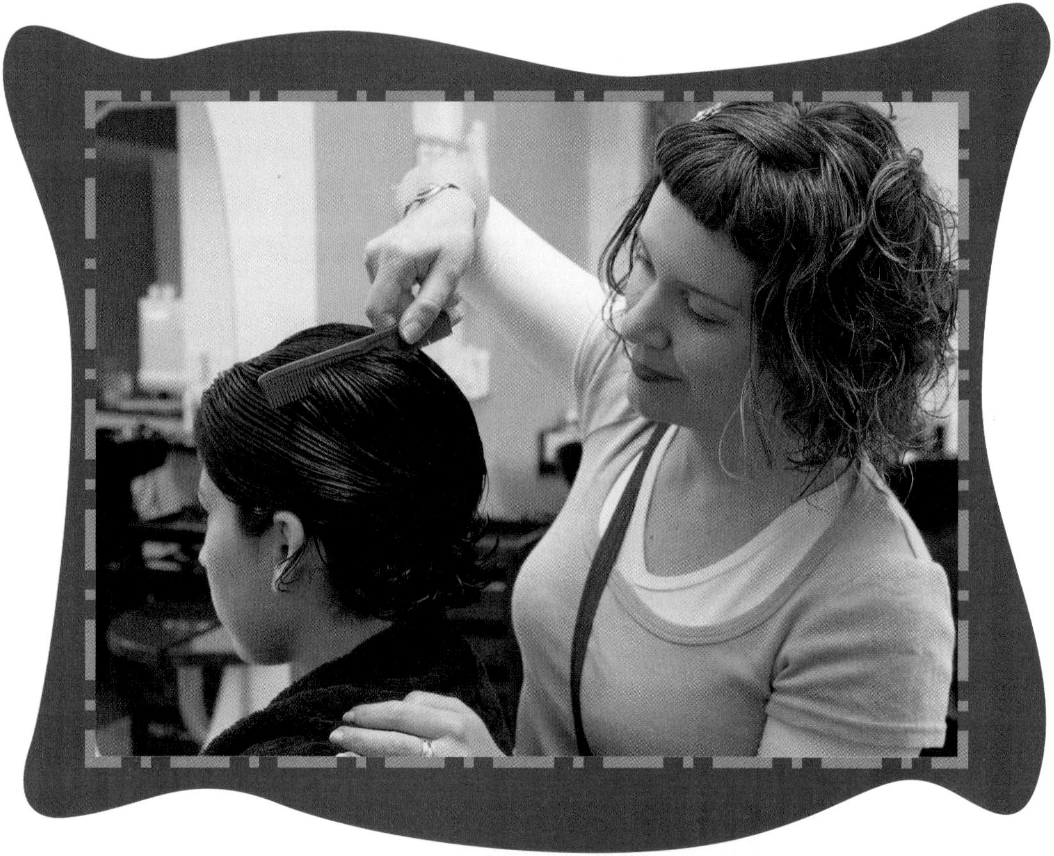

I use clips.

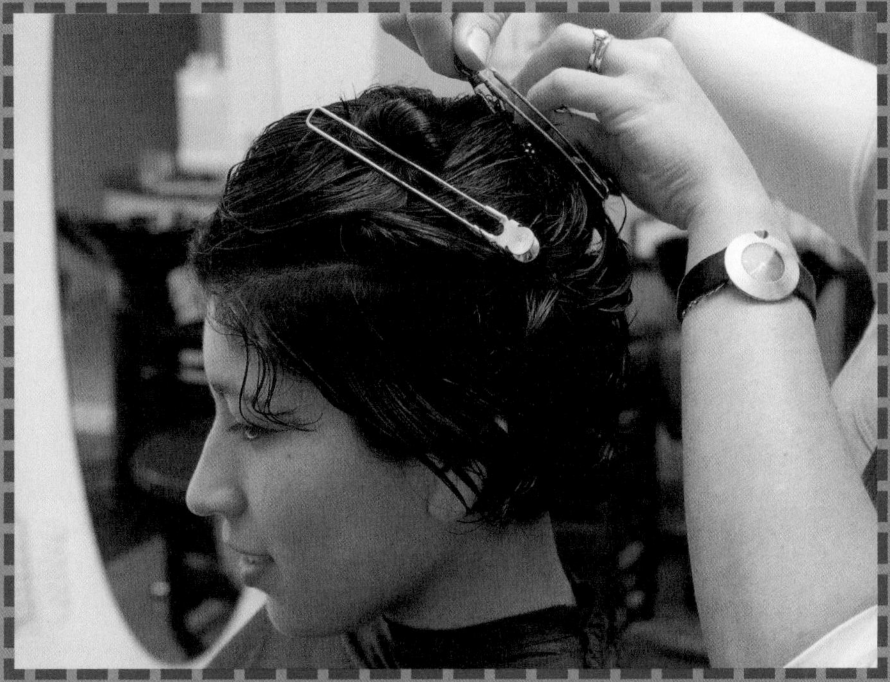

I use scissors.

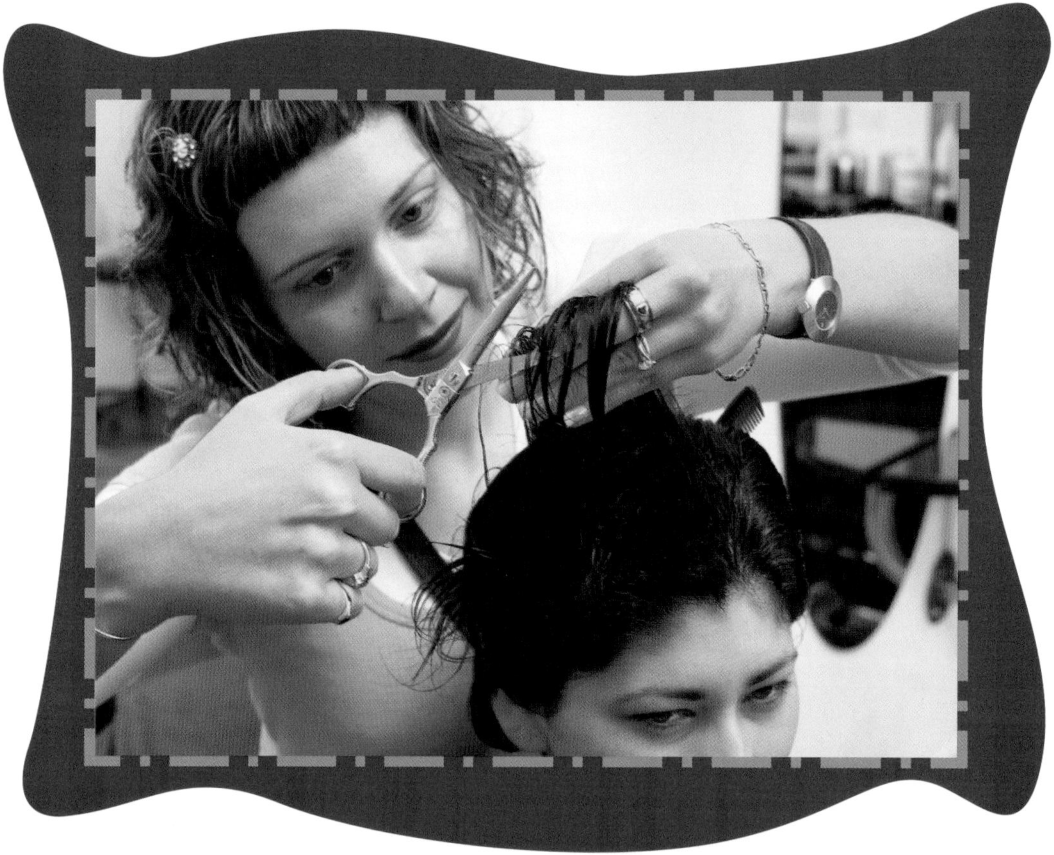

I use **clippers**.

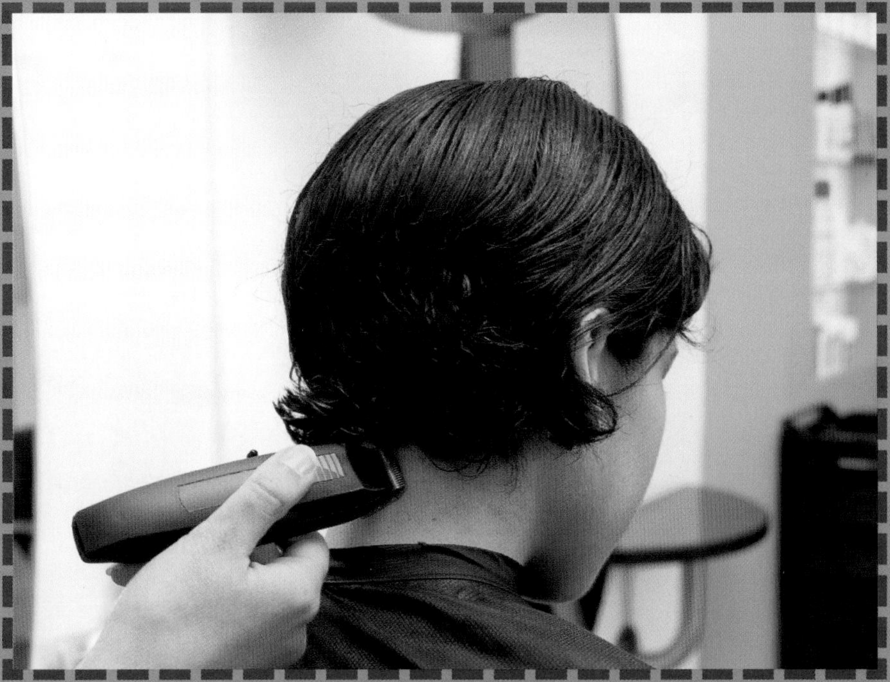

I use a hair dryer.

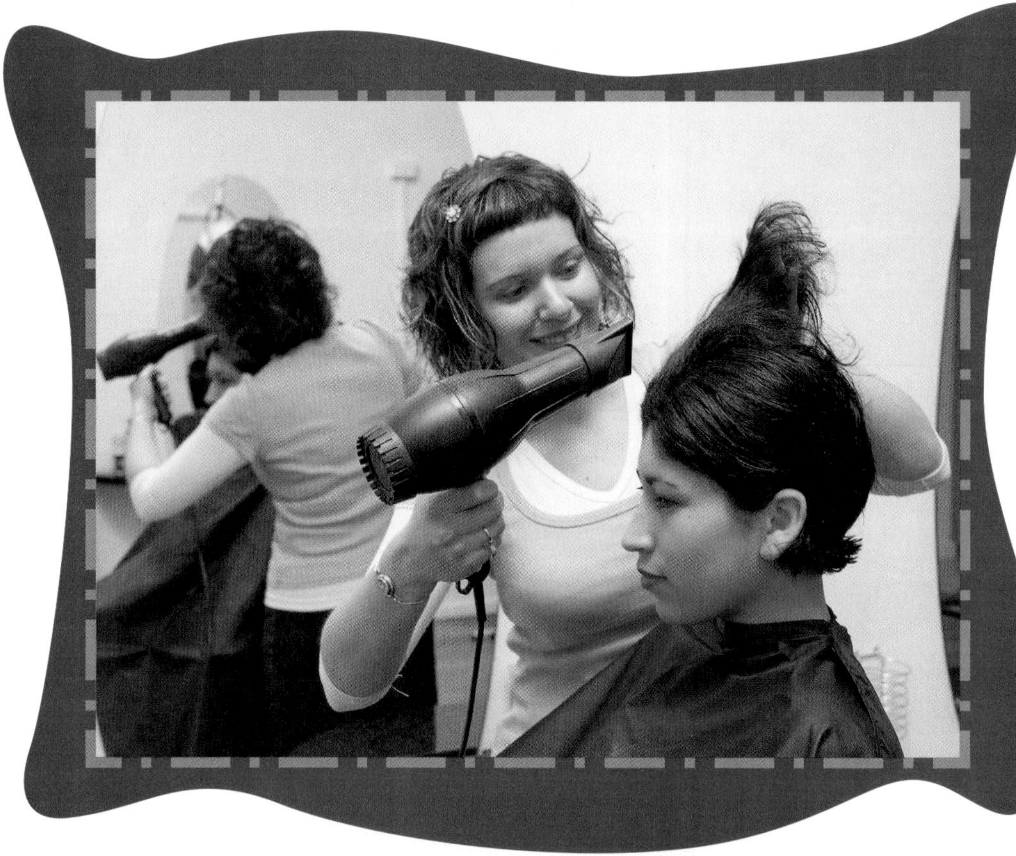

I use a **brush**.

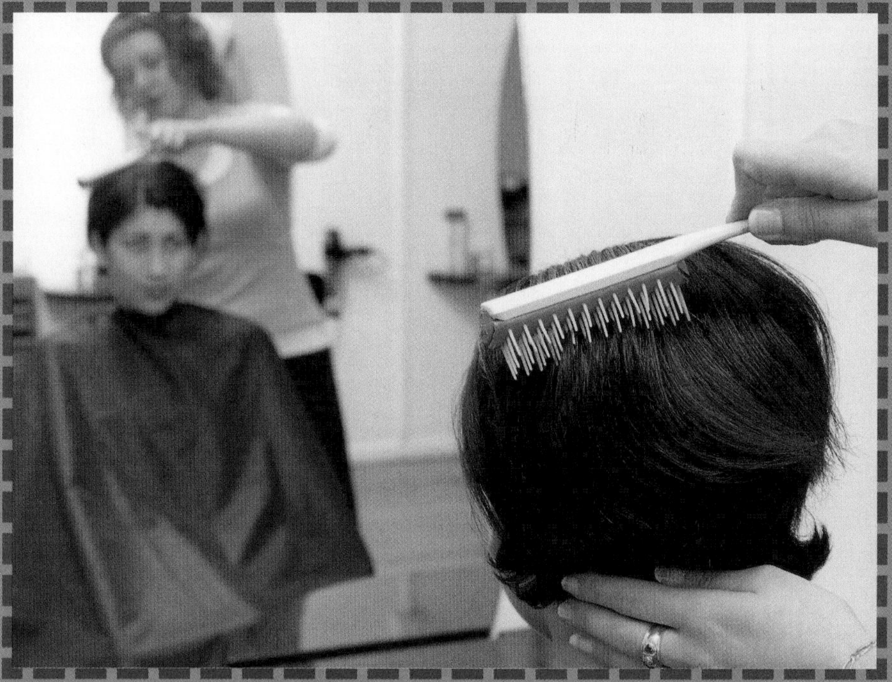

What's my job?

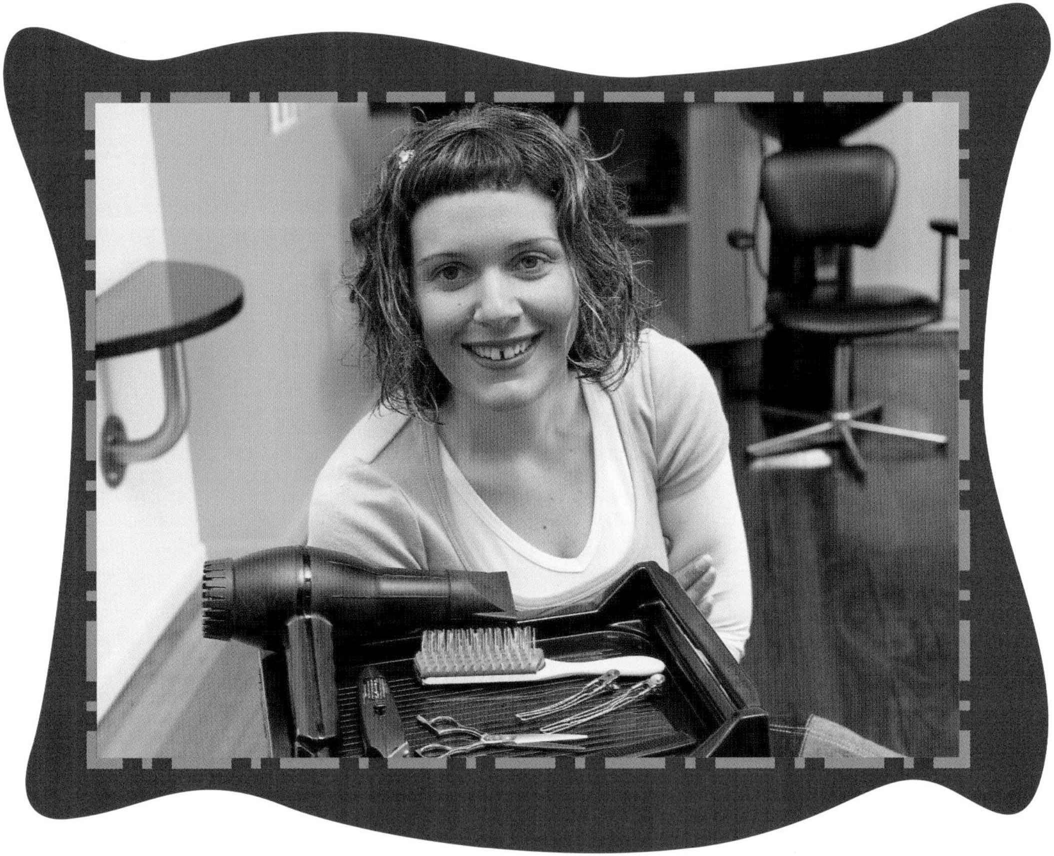